W9-BVD-606

TECHNICAL SUPPORT

Cavendish
Square
New York

Rachel
King

Published in 2015 by Cavendish Square Publishing, LLC
243 5th Avenue, Suite 136, New York, NY 10016

Website: cavendishsq.com

This publication represents the opinions and views of the author based on his or her personal experience, knowledge, and research. The information in this book serves as a general guide only. The author and publisher have used their best efforts in preparing this book and disclaim liability rising directly or indirectly from the use and application of this book.

CPSIA Compliance Information: Batch #WW15CSQ

All websites were available and accurate when this book was sent to press.

Library of Congress Cataloging-in-Publication Data

King, Rachel (Children's book author)
Technical support / Rachel King.
pages cm. — (High-tech jobs)
Includes bibliographical references and index.
ISBN 978-1-50260-114-8 (hardcover) ISBN 978-1-50260-116-2 (ebook)
1. Computer technical support—Vocational guidance—Juvenile literature. I. Title.

QA76.9.T43K495 2015
004.068'8—dc23

2014026389

Editor: Kristen Susienka
Copy Editor: Cynthia Roby
Art Director: Jeffrey Talbot
Senior Designer: Amy Greenan
Senior Production Manager: Jennifer Ryder-Talbot
Production Editor: David McNamara
Photo Researcher: J8 Media

The photographs in this book are used by permission and through the courtesy of: Cover photo and throughout, Trifonenko Ivan. Orsk/Shutterstock.com; Cover photo and 1, Flegere/Shutterstock.com; rvlsoft/Shutterstock. com, 4; Djomas/Shutterstock.com, 6; Wavebreakmedia Ltd/Wavebreak Media/Thinkstock, 9; John Fedele/ Blend Images/Getty Images, 10; Unidentified U.S. Army photographer/Historic Computer Images/File:Two women operating ENIAC (full resolution).jpg/Wikimedia Commons, 13; Rama & Musée Bolo/File:Apple II IMG 4218-black.jpg/Wikimedia Commons, 15; scyther5/Shutterstock.com, 17; Garry Knight/File:Motorola 4500X.jpg/Wikimedia Commons, 18; Cavan Images/Iconica/Getty Images, 20; Andresr/Shutterstock.com, 22; Baran azdemir/E+/Getty Images, 25; nilovsergey/Shutterstock.com, 27; ilyast/iStock/Thinkstock, 28; Air Images/Shutterstock, 33; Xavier Arnau/E+/Getty Images, 35; bikeriderlondon/Shutterstock.com, 38; Goodluz/ Shutterstock.com, 41; Todd Davidson/Illustration Works/Getty Images, 47; joyfull/Shutterstock.com, 48; © iStockphoto.com/laflor, 51; Purestock/Getty Images, 55; Twonix Studio/Shutterstock.com, 57; Raw Group/ Shutterstock.com, 59; ruxpriencdiam/Shutterstock.com, 60; DrAfter123/Vetta/Getty Images, 63; © Google/ Connie Zhou/AP Images, 64–65; bikeriderlondon/Shutterstock.com, 66; AndreyPopov/iStock/Thinkstock, 68; SpinyAnt/Shutterstock.com, 71; zimmytws/Shutterstock.com, 73; Robert Nickelsberg/Getty Images, 75; Goran Bogicevic/Shutterstock.com, 76; Goodluz/Shutterstock.com, 79.

Printed in the United States of America

CONTENTS

Tech support can be a challenging and rewarding career.

INTRODUCTION TO TECHNICAL SUPPORT

o you want to go into the technology industry but aren't sure where to start? Chances are, a good place to "get your feet wet" is in technical support. Tech support encompasses a broad range of jobs with various responsibilities. However, in general, people who work in tech support all have a similar goal. They provide answers and fix computer problems for people who use technology. A user could contact tech support if a device is broken, such as if their cell phone isn't turning on, or their computer cannot connect to the Internet. Someone might also call tech support if they want a better solution to something they already do on a regular basis, such as learning how to create formulas in Excel so they can automate calculations. Fixing computer problems might mean changing a setting in a program, or it might mean solving **hardware** problems by replacing a part of the computer itself.

Most companies provide tech support over the telephone.

There are many ways to contact tech support. Many companies provide walk-in tech support, where users can go to a designated place and get answers in person. Almost every company that provides tech support will be available by telephone, but often there will also be e-mail service. If a user wants to resolve issues themselves, many companies provide information on their website in the form of basic questions and answers, or a Frequently Asked Questions page. Tech support departments are often responsible for these do-it-yourself web pages in addition to interacting directly with users.

"HOW CAN I HELP YOU?"

Tech support is a type of customer service. Like all customer service jobs, tech support employees are first concerned with making sure the customer has a positive experience. In tech support, this means employees need to correctly diagnose the customer's issue, and then find a way to fix it. These two parts of the job require very different skills and are challenging in their own ways.

In order to correctly diagnose an issue, the employee first needs to understand the user's method of communication. This can be difficult, as the user may not understand the issue, or may not be able to describe it using precise technical vocabulary. The employee needs to be able to successfully adapt to the user's communication style. Most importantly, employees can't make assumptions about what the user is trying to tell them.

After the employee has successfully diagnosed a problem, they need to solve it. Where diagnosing the problem is challenging because it requires successful communication, solving problems is challenging because it requires troubleshooting skills. Troubleshooting is a trial-and-error process that involves testing many possible solutions before discovering one that actually solves the problem. Troubleshooting is a game of research and educated guessing, where an employee must find possible solutions through resources, such as Google, internal **documentation**, and their own previous experience, and apply those solutions in order to solve the issue in a timely manner.

WHEN DID TECH SUPPORT GET SO IMPORTANT?

Throughout the twentieth and twenty-first centuries, people invented many personal technologies for everyone to buy and use. First came telephones, then television, then later, home computers. With each advancement came different problems. Things became even more complicated when these technologies became **networked**. Phone companies and Internet service providers had to start supporting network issues, in addition to manufacturers supporting individual phone or computer issues. As the number of technologies and networks grew, having a tech support team gained importance. For example, if your cell phone, iPhone, laptop, or cable television service experiences trouble, you would have to contact the individual provider. Of course, that gets complicated! If your cell phone stops working, how do you know if you need to talk to your cell phone service provider or the company that manufactured the phone? Companies need tech support employees who know how to differentiate problems such as this, and send users in the right direction for more help.

We depend on technology to perform a lot of tasks. This dependency has led to a high demand for new technologies and technical support. Any technology company that sells hardware, such as Apple or Dell, or **software**, such as computer programs like games or antivirus software, needs a way to answer users' questions and address their complaints. Since computers have become so prevalent and relied upon for a variety of tasks, many other industries hire their own internal tech support team.

Large tech companies with many users, such as Microsoft, Apple, and AT&T, need correspondingly large technical support departments. Tech companies rely on customers to buy their products and services, so they need happy customers who will return to the same company in the future. Tech support employees are a fundamental part of making sure customers have a good experience using the technology. As a result, tech support skills are highly desirable and very transferrable. Someone with tech support skills will have many diverse job and career opportunities.

A good tech support employee should have a balance between customer service skills, such as communication and empathy with the user, and technical skills to know how to resolve an issue. They also need to be interested in puzzles. Every issue that arises is a new puzzle to solve, and some puzzles are harder than others. Tech support staff also should be adaptable. Technologies rapidly change and someone will always need to help customers use them.

This book will give you an idea of what you'll need to know about careers in tech support, including what a typical day in tech support involves, what sort of experience you'll need for different tech support jobs, and what salary and benefits you can expect. Tech support is a challenging, dynamic, and interesting career, so read on to learn more!

"

You've got to start with the customer experience and work backwards to the technology ... As we have tried to come up with a strategy and a vision for Apple, it started with 'What incredible benefits can we give to the customer? Where can we take the customer?' ... I think that's the right path to take.

STEVE JOBS, CO-FOUNDER AND
PREVIOUS CEO OF APPLE

Tech support is a challenging and interesting mix of people and technical skills.

Technical Support

1 WHAT IS TECH SUPPORT?

sing computers and other devices can at times be overwhelming. Thankfully, you don't have to go through it alone. Tech support employees are there to help customers navigate the problem-solving process. Since tech support is a subset, or type, of customer service, the primary goal is to make sure the customer has a great experience. It's not always easy. People in tech support roles are required to have patience, excellent communication skills, and the ability to adapt and learn a variety of ever-evolving technologies quickly. However, it's a job that is also rewarding!

THE HISTORY OF THE PERSONAL COMPUTER

Tech support became a feasible career path when computers finally evolved into personal computers for individuals. The computer's history is important to the way tech support has evolved. In 1946, the United States Army revealed the

Electronic Numerical Integrator and Computer (ENIAC), the first programmable general-purpose electronic digital computer. Before that, computers were **analog** and were programmed by hand using many switches and dials. The digital computer could be programmed by digital switches where "on" is coded as a one and "off" is coded as a zero. The first digital computers, including ENIAC, were designed during World War II to crack enemy codes. While ENIAC looked nothing like today's modern computers, some features of the first digital computer evolved with it, such as a **binary** system of on and off switches, and **modular** design.

Prior to ENIAC, analog computers required specialized knowledge to use them. All early programmers had to be specially trained before they could use the computers. So in the beginning, computers were much like the early automobile. They were limited to only the few people who had the knowledge to use them. As a result, there was no need for technical support. If someone was allowed to use the computer, they knew what they were doing. However, digital computers changed all of that.

When they were first invented, digital computers were just as large as analog computers, which took up entire rooms, but they quickly shrank in size. The first personal digital computers were about the size of a couch, sometimes larger. In 1957, International Business Machines (IBM) released the IBM 610, which is considered the first personal computer because it was designed for one-person operation. It wasn't intended for home use, but for computing sophisticated math in an office. It was programmed by punching holes in paper fed through the computer. Crucially, it was designed so that the operator didn't need previous programming experience to use it. All you needed was to know how to use a desk calculator. Since anyone could use the IBM 610, it marked the move away from needing special training to use computers.

For all of its advancements, the IBM 610 had its limitations. It took so long to develop that it was nearly obsolete when it was finally released. The IBM 610 also cost $55,000, putting it far out

Two women operate ENIAC, the first general-purpose digital computer.

of the price range of any individual home user. Very few units were sold. Since it wasn't very popular, IBM didn't have to worry about tech support on a large scale.

It took a while for computer prices to decrease enough so that more people could afford them. A lower price also meant changes to the computer's appearance. First, some of the larger, more unwieldy parts were replaced with more efficient, smaller parts. People then began buying those parts individually and assembling computers in their basements. Thus the personal computer movement was, at the start, "do-it-yourself." This is how the first Apple computer was created in 1976.

As Apple and other personal computers became more popular, more affordable, and reached wider audiences, managers realized that tech support was becoming a vital resource for users. The computers, however, were so complicated and open-ended that both sellers and users were constantly confused by their operation, even though they came with extensive instructions. The problem, of course, was that like a lot of technical documentation, the Apple user manual and other explanatory documents were difficult to understand and much of its vocabulary was unfamiliar to users. In 1980, Apple set up a tech support hotline for their sellers to ask questions. They expected the sellers to then interact with customers, and answer the customers' questions. Yet even the people selling Apple computers were confused when it came to its manuals. Only 12 percent of the hotline calls were for questions not already answered in Apple's documentation.

The lack of user-friendly documentation for early computers opened a market for easy-to-read, third-party explanations. Some companies started publishing books and magazines about how to use computers and troubleshoot them when they had problems. Users created support networks with their own mailing lists and groups that met to talk about computers. The computer companies hadn't done a good enough job of making their products easy to understand, so others filled the demand with a variety of supplementary resources. Just as the first computers were do-it-yourself, so was the first tech support.

Companies quickly realized that customers needed specialized employees to help customers understand the product and its documentation. There were a lot of benefits for companies to provide that support themselves instead of depending on third-party and informal support. For instance, by providing their own tech support services, companies could increase customer happiness and loyalty, learn about recurring issues and fix them in later updates, and charge for support.

Tech support offers a guide to a product and a user's understanding of it. By speaking directly to a customer, employees personalize the experience and adapt to individual customers' needs and technical knowledge. These employees also translate heavy technology jargon into terms a customer can easily understand. Tech support not only allows companies to help people use their products, it also gives them an opportunity to make

their customers happier, which brings them back in the future. For example, today's Apple's Genius Bar tech support employees are trained to focus on repairing the customer's relationship with the technology and Apple itself. For those employees, making the customers happy is far more important than immediately fixing the problem. Apple and other computer companies dedicate a tremendous amount of resources to tech support, as that is a valuable element to the success of their business.

WHY ARE COMPUTERS SO DIFFICULT?

If computers are so confusing, then why have they grown so popular? Although it wasn't clear to everyone at the beginning, computers are immensely powerful. Spreadsheet and word processing applications were invented in the 1980s. For many, these applications finally demonstrated the usefulness of a computer because people could do things on a computer far faster than they'd ever been able to do by hand. It took a lot of practice to do it well, though, as there weren't any mice or clickable

> ❝ ❞
> *As early as 1980 an Apple Computer executive observed that one of the areas that will have the greatest impact in selling computers is the quality of after-sale support a firm can deliver.*

JOSEPH J. CORN,
STANFORD HISTORY PROFESSOR

icons onscreen. Instead, users did everything with a keyboard. The process was difficult but rewarding.

As with each new technology, people had to conquer a learning curve. Many other technologies, such as electric mixers or gas-powered lawnmowers, had been automated versions of already-existing machines. Other inventions, such as telephones and radios, were intuitive to use because they had limited functionality and were more user friendly. Any problems with such devices were typically hardware related, or trouble with the radio signal or phone network. Since hardware and networks needed specialized tools and parts, experts were always needed to fix them. However, not all inventions were so straightforward.

The car, for instance, was confusing from the start because it relied on several different parts. Operating cars was especially

```
  3   }
  4
 55   ▣ function updatePhotoDescription() {
 56     ▣    if (descriptions.length > (page * 9) + (currentImage substring()-1)(
_57          document.getElementById(bigImageDesc).innerHTML = descriptions(se
258     }
259   }
260
261   ▣ function updateAllImages() {
262        var i = 1;
263   ▣    while (i < 10) {
264            var elementId = 'foto' + i;
265            var elementIdBig = 'bigImage' + i;
266   ▣        if (page * 9 + i - 1 < photos.length) {
267                document.getElementById( elementId ).src = 'images/thm' + i
268                document.getElementById( elementIdBig ).src = 'images/
269            } else {
270                document.getElementById( elementId ).src = '';
```

Computers are incredibly powerful because they can be programmed (shown here) to do a variety of tasks.

challenging when they were a new technology, but even now states require drivers to take and pass a test before they can drive alone. Although car travel is more widely accessible to the public, as opposed to, say, flying a plane, users are expected to know certain rules before driving.

In terms of user friendliness, computers were even worse than cars. First, they were abstract. While a car's functionality was hidden under a hood, it was not even visible in a computer. This is still the case today. Everything that happens inside a computer is due to electrical currents, and you can't open one up while it's running to determine what each part does. You can't see a computer save information to its hard drive, or watch the mechanical parts run a program. In turn, this made, and still makes, them very difficult to understand.

This cell phone from the 1980s is an example of how quickly technologies can change over a few decades.

Second, computer vocabulary was more confusing than the new vocabulary customers had to learn when cars became widespread. Car vocabulary is quite different than anything else, because it refers to the mechanics of motors. Computers have their own technical vocabulary, too. You can discuss hardware and software, or use networking terms, such as modem and Ethernet. Computers also have a lot of technical terms that are acronyms, like RAM. They also redefine already-existing words and give them technical meanings.

Third, computers change far more frequently than cars. As a result, computers become outdated faster, unlike other technological advances. For example, a thirty-year-old car still has value and can be used for its original purpose. A thirty-year-old computer, however, isn't good for much except a museum. Current technology, such as laptops, smartphones, and tablets, continue this trend. The technology has changed rapidly.

Not only do computers change from one model to the next, but they've also evolved substantially over time. While the first computers were large enough to take up an entire room, or two, they've now gotten small enough to fit inside a pocket, as is the case with a smartphone. Smartphones, tablets, and desktop computers all provide different user experiences and have their own quirks. As a result, they all need their own tech support. Some tech support employees are responsible for supporting a variety of devices, which requires adaptability and flexibility.

Lastly, computers are open-ended, meaning they can be used for multiple purposes. An electric mixer mixes. A lawnmower mows the lawn. Even a car has only one purpose, to transport people from one point to another. Yet a computer can be used to write a text document or calculate data in a spreadsheet, or use a **browser** to surf the Internet. E-mail has become a fundamental method of communication. Computers are used for these purposes every day by millions of people. If you know how, you can even write your own programs that will tell the computer what to do. This opens up a lot of possibilities. It can, however, make things more difficult; "unlimited possibilities" can also mean almost "unlimited problems." Even from the beginning, vendors and users came up with support systems for when they had questions and problems.

Of course, the fact that computers are so open-ended works in their favor. We rely on computers to perform a variety of tasks because they can. Companies do most, if not all, of their bookkeeping with computers, such as employee time entry, budgeting, and storing customer information. Researchers use computers to collect data and find patterns in massive amounts of data. For example, the Mars rovers are computers, and were programmed using other computers. Stores use computers to run their sales systems and update inventory. The invention of tablets has made a huge impact on small businesses, as they can now use tablets to keep track of sales and charge customers far more cheaply and flexibly than they could with a desktop computer. Tech support can help with all of these uses.

We use computers for a variety of purposes, and more uses will come as computers and their different versions become more powerful. They'll get smaller, which means they'll become even more integrated into our daily lives. Computers will

Using Square allows small businesses to charge customers' credit cards through a tablet like the iPad.

become wearable. They'll begin imitating and interacting with our three-dimensional world, instead of being confined to two-dimensional screens. Many more devices will connect to the Internet. As computers evolve, tech support will evolve with them.

THE MANY FACETS OF TECH SUPPORT

People learn in different ways. In the late 1970s, Microsoft started investigating the types of support people might need to use their products. They discovered that there were often cultural differences in how people learned best. Users in some countries preferred to be taught by another person, or to read the manual. In the United States, most people would often ignore the manual or documentation that came with a computer or a piece of software. Instead, they'd learn by trying, and then would look for an answer if they got stuck.

> # " "
>
> *I think it's fair to say that personal computers have become the most empowering tool we've ever created. They're tools of communication, they're tools of creativity, and they can be shaped by their user.*

BILL GATES, CO-FOUNDER AND CEO OF MICROSOFT

As a result, companies have always tried to provide support in a variety of ways. Telephone call centers have been around since the 1960s, and 1-800 numbers were invented in 1967. In the late 1970s, Interactive Voice Responses (IVRs) started allowing companies to create automated "phone tree" menus to redirect users to the correct department. IVRs are what allow computers to interact with humans over the phone, requiring the caller to press a number on the keypad or use a voice command to indicate the type of question they have. With all of these new phone technologies, more companies could open call centers and support their customers that way.

In the mid-1990s, when using the Internet became more common, e-mail and live chats became viable support options as well. As computers and network connections have become faster, remote support software has also become a possible way to provide tech support. With remote support software, a tech support employee can remotely access a user's computer and repair issues without needing to physically visit the computer or have it brought in for service.

Behind the scenes, a tech support employee will take down information about a user and his or her computer, such as its brand and operating system, and how long the problem has occurred. The employee will then do some research on what the problem might be. Tech support departments usually have access to **knowledge bases**, databases full of questions and solutions. They reference these first when a user has a question they haven't encountered before. Knowledge bases have been around, in one form or another, since before 1985 and are still commonly used today.

Some companies offer live chat tech support.

Of course, it's even better if you can eliminate a lot of the issues that occur for more than one user. Many people call with the same question, so companies monitor what sorts of questions are being asked. Using this information, they try to fix these **bugs**, or common problems, in the next computer or software version. Some companies even require the programmers and engineers making the product to spend some time doing tech support so that they can hear firsthand what sorts of areas are causing problems. Then the programmers can go back and fix bugs and make the product more user friendly so less people ask how to use it. This allows the tech support team to focus on other issues, such as teaching users how to use new tools and features.

Tech support has evolved along with computer advancements. The first computers didn't have hard drives, so every time they were turned off, or they lost power accidentally, the operating system had to be reinstalled. To access a specific program required a **floppy disk** or other external storage. This also meant that all data had to be saved to external storage. If you'd written a document, for example, you then had to save it on a floppy. To do this, sometimes technical support teams were consulted. Over the years, things have become simpler. Computers now have Graphical User Interfaces (GUIs), which allow users to click menus and buttons onscreen with a mouse, instead of having to memorize the precise and unforgiving computer language previously used as a computer command. Users can also save their documents directly to the computer or using USBs or cloud devices. These features have come about as a result of tech support and computer engineers working together to make computers more intuitive and easier to use.

TECH SUPPORT TODAY

Today, there are three major divisions of tech support: network, hardware, and software. People generally specialize in one depending on their interests as well as public demand.

There are people who only support the networks that computers use to pass along information. These people, called network technicians, often work for Internet service providers (ISPs), who sell Internet subscriptions. Some common ISPs are Comcast, AT&T, and CenturyLink. Network technicians also work for individual companies that are large enough to need their own internal networks. A network tech makes sure that the network runs smoothly, and works constantly to make it secure and efficient. Network techs usually work behind the scenes and don't necessarily interact with customers. Unless something is physically wrong with the network, they can often work remotely.

The Tiers of Tech Support

Depending on its size, a tech support department can include multiple levels of support. Most have one or two tiers, and sometimes three. The different tiers require different skill sets and encourage a variety of experience levels. The lowest tier, tier one, is entry-level. The upper tiers require more experience. Departments with multiple tiers of support accommodate beginners and allow for career advancement.

Tier one is primarily responsible for intake, or directing calls. People working in tier one will be the first point of contact for a customer. He or she will do most of the initial communication with the user and will try to determine the issue the user is facing. People in this tier must be effective communicators, since they spend the majority of their time interacting with customers, but they don't necessarily need to know how to resolve issues. Tier one must act as the filter to the rest of tech support. Their primary responsibility is ensuring issues are directed to someone who can solve them. Often these people are in tier two.

Once the user's issue is relayed to them, tier two employees will troubleshoot to find a satisfactory solution. Tier two employees must have excellent troubleshooting skills, but don't need to interact with users as much. Tier two must be adaptable and resourceful, as they'll often encounter problems and devices they aren't experienced with and will need to find information and successfully troubleshoot.

Some companies also offer tier three support. If this is the case, tier two will typically perform a certain level of troubleshooting. There's often a general rule of thumb: "If the

problem can be solved in fifteen minutes, it's a tier two issue."
Tier three, however, is the expert level. These employees are
the ones who deal with the most complicated and sophisticated
issues. These issues are the ones that are uncommon, time-
consuming, or both. Tier three employees are also the most
specialized. Generally, each employee specializes in a different
area, so the department can cover many different types of
problems. Tier three employees are curious and driven to learn
as much as possible about the products they support.

If the company makes computers or software, tier three
support can also work with engineers and programmers to fix
issues before the next product release. This also requires a fair
amount of expertise, as these support employees will have to be
very familiar with the product in order to offer suggestions. Since
tier three employees are the most technically savvy support
employees, their experiences with how customers interact with
the technology are invaluable to the rest of the tech staff. All the
tiers, especially tier three, have an important perspective on the
user experience.

Hardware technicians also tend to work behind the scenes, from a specialized workstation called a tech bench. Hardware technicians solve hardware problems, so they need a variety of tools and spare parts stocked at their workstations, depending on the types of computers they're expected to fix. Although hardware techs do go out in the field, if a piece of hardware is irreparably broken, they'll often need to bring the computer back to their tech bench to replace it. If your hard drive fails, for example, a hardware tech will replace it with a new one. Hardware techs can also run automatic hardware tests to figure out what part is having problems.

Software technicians, usually called desktop support, interact most with customers. Typically, desktop support is the department you contact when you experience an issue. If the issue is software related, such as a program that's not installing properly or an incorrect setting, they may be able to repair it. If a network or hardware tech needs to address the problem, the person receiving phone calls will route the issue to them.

Tech support can vary in other ways as well. For example, many companies that sell hardware or software have their own tech support departments to assist customers who use their products, whereas non-tech companies have in-house Information Technology (IT) departments, which are responsible for that company's network and computers, and also help their own users with computer issues. In-house tech support can often include a help desk dedicated to internal users. In-house tech support and tech support provided as part of customer service can have very different priorities. Both levels of tech support, however, can only support certain technologies. For example, you can't contact Microsoft's tech support when you're having a hardware problem with an Apple computer. Likewise, in-house tech support often has specific limitations on the company-provided software and hardware they can help fix.

DOCUMENTATION

Most regular tech support positions are reactive, meaning they wait for customers to ask them for help. They then do their best to resolve the issue. Sometimes, however, part of a tech support employee's job is documentation, meaning the creation of any kind of explanation of a product. Documentation can include instructions on how to use a product, such as a manual, and information on how to troubleshoot product issues. Although it's not usually available to the public, documentation can also include how the product was made.

Unlike most of tech support, documentation is proactive. You write documentation before someone might need it, so you can later access it quickly. It's not part of every tech support employee's job. Most tech support employees will use the documentation as resources, without being required to help create it. Documentation as a whole, however, is closely tied to tech support. Both are dedicated to helping customers use the product properly.

Many devices and applications have built-in help menus and help keys (such as F1). These are helpful when a user experiences difficulties locating a specific menu or getting the device or application to perform a specific task. It's not perfect, of course. Thus tech support exists to address the questions help menus and manuals can't, and to give personalized help for individual problems.

Tech support employees act as the bridge between technology and users, helping customers get the most from their computers. Tech support can also tailor the experience to a customer's specific needs. In the next chapter, you'll read about how to prepare for a career in tech support, and learn more about the types of skills someone in tech support should have.

Jobs **Find your career**

Careers in technology

There are a variety of ways you can gain the experience necessary for a tech support career.

ork Administrator. Includes links to ministrato's &st by companies that ators.

What a Software Quality Assurance team does. Education, Training and certifications to get a job as a Software Quality Assurance Engineer. How to find a job as a Software Quality

Patience, endurance, and a machines function will bene programming. These tech-s

2 GETTING A CAREER IN THE FIELD

The three main tech support divisions, network, hardware, and software, have slightly different job requirements. Required education, training, and previous experience will vary depending on the type of tech support you want to do, but a lot of skills requirements overlap between the three divisions. You'll need certain tools, such as a technology-related degree, relevant work or volunteer experience, and maybe some industry **certifications**, regardless of what sort of tech job you're interested in. Below we'll explore the qualifications you'll need for a job in tech support.

EDUCATION

Although entry-level tech support jobs, such as help desk technician or other tier-one positions, won't necessarily require any higher education, many upper-level tech support jobs, such as tier-three support, require an associate's (two year) or a bachelor's (four year) degree. In general, you should get a degree if you can. Having one will make you more attractive to potential employers, and you will gain an edge over your competition.

There are two common associate's and bachelor's degrees most people in the tech industry receive: computer science and information technology (IT). Computer science degrees are geared toward people who want to know how software works and how to create it. If you like knowing how a computer translates a user's input into the computer language of ones and zeroes and building programs that tell the computer exactly what to do, this might be a good degree for you. Typically, computer science classes will revolve around how to program in several different types of programming languages, how computers talk to each other over a network, and how to create better **algorithms**. Since software relies heavily on math, a computer science degree will also require a lot of math. Be prepared to take math classes for the majority of your years at college if you want to earn a bachelor's in computer science. People going for an IT degree, on the other hand, usually enjoy fixing things on the physical computer, or on programs running on the computer. An IT degree tends to focus on using existing hardware and software to get things done. There is some overlap between the two degrees, of course. For example, both degrees will have classes about networks, but IT network classes will focus on the practicalities of creating and maintaining a computer network, while computer science's focus will be on how computers use software to talk to each other over a network. IT will also have classes on how databases work, how to repair hardware and software, and security policy.

There's a third option for computer-related degrees, a degree in computer engineering. Like other types of engineering, computer engineering is dedicated to using science and technology to improve and create products. In a computer engineer's case, the "products" are computers. Computer engineers create new computer parts that work when assembled.

Computer engineering degrees exist, but tech support jobs don't require them, so we won't go into further detail about them here.

While your first entry-level tech support job may not require any higher education, you may have difficulties after that without one. Associate's and bachelor's degrees are becoming increasingly expected for jobs in many different industries, including technology. A computer-related degree indicates that you're serious about pursuing a computer-related career, that you have the dedication and motivation to handle long-term projects, and that you have demonstrated a certain level of knowledge. It also means that you're good at learning new information. These are all vital qualities that employers seek. As a result, a bachelor's degree in information technology or a related field (such as computer science or information security) is a very important qualification.

That being said, a degree is best supplemented with work experience. In addition, it is possible, although it can be difficult, to get tech support and other IT jobs without higher education. Instead, you'll need extensive practical experience and skills, and certifications, in order to demonstrate a thorough understanding of computers and computer problems. However, having a degree tells potential employers that you have all the qualifications mentioned above, so it is highly recommended.

TRAINING

Since degrees aren't always required for tech support jobs, many people get certifications instead of, or in addition to, a degree. Certifications prove that you know a specific skill very well. There are many types of certifications available for various skills. Typically, you take an exam (or two) and have to get a specific grade to pass and receive the certification. You can take training classes through various companies, or find study books to prepare yourself for the exam.

So what types of certifications are available, and which ones are the most useful? As with everything else, context

The College Search

Do you want to earn a computer-related degree but aren't sure where to start looking for colleges? If you think an information technology degree would be the best fit for you, you'll want to consult specific college resources, such as the College Board website (bigfuture.collegeboard.org). Information technology degrees are a bit specialized, so you should search for colleges by major. If you're most interested in a computer science degree, the process is a little different. Computer science degree programs are easy to find—almost any four-year college has one. If this is what you're looking for, your college search will be much the same as for any other degree.

The most prestigious colleges for computer science are technical schools, such as Massachusetts Institute of Technology (MIT), California Institute of Technology (Caltech), and Carnegie Mellon University. The United Kingdom's top higher education magazine, *The Times Higher Education*, ranks the top 100 international universities in engineering and technology every year (timeshighereducation.co.uk/world-university-rankings/2013-14/subject-ranking/subject/engineering-and-IT). Approximately a third of the colleges on the list are in the United States.

Rankings are interesting, but there's far more to choosing a college. Regardless of the type of degree you're interested in, there are a few other things you should consider. Price is definitely an important factor. Attending a public university or an in-state community college are the most affordable options. The school's size is another thing you should consider. Private liberal arts colleges are more expensive than public schools, but tend to have fewer students and have smaller class sizes. As a result, the experience at a small school is more personal, and you'll have more opportunities for one-on-one interaction with your instructors. Location is also important. Where do you want to live for four years?

These are ultimately deal breakers when you are deciding where you'd like to attend college (major, price, size, and location). There are plenty of college search books and websites available to guide you. Your guidance counselor may have resources to help with your search, and there is also a list in the Further Information section at the back of this book.

is important. Different companies and job titles will require different certifications. Below is an introduction to the types of certificates you can get in the tech industry.

COMPTIA CERTIFICATIONS

- A+ Certification: One of the most universally recognized certifications, A+ has two required exams. A+ tests both hardware and software troubleshooting skills, as well as networking connectivity troubleshooting and the basics of Android and iOS. It's required for official Dell, Lenovo, and Intel technicians.

- Network+: Recommended for anyone interested in network support, Network+ tests your ability to set up and maintain computer networks. This includes familiarity with the actual hardware of a network, as well as security and configuring networks to run smoothly.

CISCO

- CCENT (Cisco Certified Entry Networking Technician): The most basic Cisco certification, it's intended for entry-level network techs. CCENT tests your basic network skills, much like the Network+, but on a simpler level. It tests your ability to install and maintain a small network, as well as some basic network security.

- CCNA (Cisco Certified Network Associate): A step above CCENT, CCNA challenges you to set up a medium-sized network. CCNA also focuses on making networks as efficient as possible.

APPLE

- ACMT (Apple Certified Macintosh Technician): Required for official Apple techs, much like the A+ is required for official Dell, Lenovo, and Intel techs.

Certifications are helpful and can give you a step up, but aren't always required. This is especially true in entry-level tech support jobs. Yet like higher education, certifications are often invaluable and sometimes required for upper-level jobs. Certifications are great ways to get ahead of your competition.

If you're interested in a career in tech support, and IT in general, the basic certifications are excellent places to start. From there, try to specialize. Are you interested in networks? Take the CCENT and CCNA. If you prefer Windows or Macs, try taking their respective certifications. If you know you like working with databases or **servers**, find a certification that focuses on those strengths.

Once you have the basics down, specialize in what interests you.

EXPERIENCE AND SKILLS

Experience is the most important qualification employers look for in potential tech support employees. Fortunately, there are many types of experiences, and also many skills unrelated to technology that jobs require.

COMMUNICATION SKILLS

Anyone in tech support will need excellent communication skills. Tech support employees must be able to communicate effectively via different methods, including phone, e-mail, or in person. First-tier tech support employees need to be able to describe the problem accurately, which requires successful communication with the customer. As mentioned earlier, customers aren't always tech-savvy, which means that you'll need to be able to communicate with them using non-technical vocabulary. You'll also need to be able to interpret what they mean, since customers will often use inaccurate words to describe the problem or what they're trying to do. It's also dangerous to make assumptions while trying to interpret what a customer is telling you. This can lead to attempts to resolve an issue that doesn't actually exist, instead of solving the real issue.

CUSTOMER SERVICE

Experience in customer service is perhaps the most important skill you can have if you're interested in tech support. Especially for entry-level jobs, being able to relate to and communicate with customers is a vital part of tech support. Customer service experience also indicates that you have communication skills, which is one of the fundamental skills necessary to succeed in any tech support job. You need to care about a customer's individual experience, and whether they get the answer they need before they leave your place of business or the call ends. Many employers agree that it's much easier to teach employees technical skills rather than people skills, so they prefer to hire based on customer service experience.

Because customer service skills aren't tech support or IT-related, you can gain them from a variety of non-technical jobs. Working in the food industry as a server or wait staff, or as a cashier in retail, are great ways to gain this experience. Even better, entry-level customer service jobs are easily available, making this an accessible skill to most people.

> **"** **"**
>
> ## When I do hiring, I definitely look for customer service [experience] ... Especially since we already have a knowledge base and a lot of documentation, it's much easier to teach the technical rather than the customer service.

SIGUCCS (SPECIAL INTEREST GROUP ON UNIVERSITY AND COLLEGE COMPUTING SERVICES) WEBINAR, "CUSTOMER SERVICE THEN AND NOW" BY ASHLEY WEESE

TROUBLESHOOTING

Troubleshooting, another vital tech support skill, is a subset of problem-solving. Tech support employees need to be able to methodically create and test hypotheses about why something

Figuring out which cables go to which devices requires troubleshooting.

isn't working. This requires the ability to research possible causes and make educated guesses about which causes best fit the symptoms. Troubleshooting, and therefore problem-solving, is typically more important for the upper tiers of support, as they are responsible for resolving the issues that tier one reports. Excellent problem-solving skills indicate that you're ready for advancement within tech support.

Although you might think that troubleshooting is a technology-specific skill, that's not necessarily true. As in the introduction, troubleshooting can be broadly defined as "a trial-and-error process that can require testing many possible solutions before discovering the one that actually solves the problem." This doesn't just apply to computers. If you've ever tried to figure out why a household appliance isn't working, you've tried to troubleshoot a problem. Troubleshooting is a thought process during which you use creative thinking to generate possible solutions and then methodically eliminate solutions that don't actually work.

Troubleshooting consists of several parts. First you have to have a good idea of what the problem is. This can be tricky, as you can't always make assumptions about what's going wrong. Also, if you're getting secondhand information from a customer, sometimes they'll make assumptions and will not relay accurate information as a result. This often makes troubleshooting more difficult, as you don't necessarily start with an accurate diagnosis of the issue.

Once you know the issue, however, you then have to have possible explanations as to "why" the problem is happening. For example, perhaps the issue is that users can't successfully log on to a website. Is their network connection not working? Is a network option on the wrong setting? Is the username or password incorrect? Part of the responsibility of the troubleshooter is to pinpoint the exact location of the error.

Ideally, you also need to be able to solve the problem, but sometimes circumstances conspire against you, and although you know what the problem is and why it's happening, you can't do anything to fix it. While situations like this are frustrating, they do occur. The next best thing is to be able to send the customer in the right direction for more help.

TECHNICAL SKILLS

You might wonder, what about actual technical computer skills? Aren't those important? Absolutely! The more comfortable you are with a variety of technologies, the better prepared you'll be for a tech support job. This can be tricky. Technologies are constantly changing, and often tech support is expected to be comfortable with a variety of hardware and operating systems. Generally, it's a good bet to tinker with anything you can get your hands on, whether it's mobile technologies, such as Android and iOS, or traditional operating systems, such as Windows and Mac. Hardware varies even more, with many PC devices having vastly different hardware beneath the surface. It's difficult to recommend just one technology that is a must-know, especially since technology changes so quickly and the primary technological focus will depend on the company providing the tech support. Because of this, it's best to generalize, at least in the beginning.

The most effective tech support employees will know a little about hardware, a little about software, and a little about networks. These basics will apply to all entry-level tech support positions, and will then lead to the ability to specialize in whichever you prefer. What are some basic tech skills you should know?

- How to get to the system preferences, also called the Control Panel
- How to get to the network settings and troubleshoot basic Ethernet (if available) and Wi-Fi issues
- How to change individual program preferences
- How to close open programs, especially if they're frozen
- How to shut down/restart

This is a very basic and generic list. Tech support is often required to assist with many different types of devices, and a lot of required information will vary from company to company. In addition, upper-level tech support positions will require even more technical skills and training.

OTHER EXPERIENCE

If you don't currently have a tech job, it can be difficult to get your first one. It seems like a difficult situation. How can you get the experience you need for a tech job if you don't have one already? Formal education, such as an associate's or bachelor's degree in information technology, and certifications are great ways to demonstrate what skills you know. However, you can learn tech skills in other ways, too.

- **MOOC**: MOOC stands for Massive Open Online Course. This is a new trend in higher education, where institutions design online classes and then open them to the public for free. The quality and time commitment varies from class to class, but you can find many tech and computer-related MOOCs on a variety of topics. In a typical MOOC, you'll watch class lectures recorded by the professor, then complete homework assignments, quizzes, and tests. Classes usually run from eight to eleven weeks. Some MOOCs provide certificates at the end of the class to students who passed. Some websites that provide MOOCs are Coursera, edX, Udacity, and Khan Academy.

Try asking an adult at your school, such as a guidance counselor or teacher, about ways to gain experience.

- **Internships**: An internship is a temporary position with an emphasis on on-the-job training rather than employment. It can be paid or unpaid. Either way, the experience gained combined with corporate exposure and contacts can be invaluable when exploring your post-internship job options. Software companies, banks, and other financial institutions offer attractive internships. To search for internship opportunities in your area, visit internships.com.

- **Meetups**: Meetup.com is a website dedicated to getting people in touch with others who share the same interests. People create groups that meet in person and have scheduled activities. For many people in the tech industry, joining a Meetup provides a support network of people who have experience and can answer questions or direct you to new resources. Meetups are a great resource to meet people who can help you with whatever you're learning about.

- **Volunteer**: There are a huge number of tech-related nonprofit companies that always need volunteers to help repair computers and teach people how to use them. Free Geek (freegeek.org) is a nonprofit that began in Portland, Oregon, and inspired other cities to start similar organizations. Free Geek accepts volunteers, and also teaches classes on a variety of computer-related subjects. World Computer Exchange (worldcomputerexchange.org) is a similar nonprofit, with locations in other cities in both the United States and Canada. For similar organizations in your area, go to idealist.com and search organizations for "computer," or visit this web page that lists different computer nonprofits: www.dmoz.org/Computers/Organizations/Non-Profit.

- **Stack Exchange**: Although there's also a lot of information on the Internet about computer support and repair, sifting through it can often be overwhelming. Stack Exchange is a collection of Q&A sites on a variety of subjects. Questions and answers are both moderated, and you can learn a lot from watching people debate possible causes of an issue and the best solution. Stack Exchange includes sites for Apple users, Unix and Linux operating systems, systems administrators, information security, and network engineers, among others. For a full list of their technology-related sites, go to stackexchange.com/sites#technology.

In addition to the resources above, your local library may have books on computer repair, as well as books dedicated to specific software or hardware. If you have a computer teacher, ask him or her for other resources as well.

WHERE TO GO FROM HERE

Tech support, in and of itself, isn't necessarily a career. However, it can be. It depends on the company you work for, and how much

" "

Microsoft always looked at support as a career and tried to hire good people and tried to develop professional support people. Our belief was that the nature of a person who does support is somebody who is friendly and who likes solving problems … The support person is a people person, a nurturer … and that doesn't change no matter how skilled you get or how experienced you are.

MIKE MAPLES SR.,
FORMER MICROSOFT MANAGER

opportunity there is for advancement. Some companies have enough people in customer service roles that they can organize the tech support division to make it a feasible career.

Many people also use tech support as a stepping-stone into the tech industry. From there, they decide where they want to go next. There are a lot of options available. Some people go into management. Some people will also start their own computer consulting companies and hire others to do the support itself while they run the company. Others choose to get more involved behind the scenes, becoming network or systems administrators, technical writers, or programmers. Tech support employees make great behind-the-scenes employees, who work on technical things like networks and servers. Tech support employees know what the customers want and what needs to be prioritized. So if they move to back-end work, they can implement those changes. They can also move into sales, because they know their product very well and can give excellent recommendations. To give you a better idea, here is more information about the most typical jobs people take after starting in tech support:

- **Management**: The most self-explanatory step beyond tech support. With management or leadership training, someone in tech support is well equipped to supervise others, especially other tech support employees. A background in tech support guarantees that an employee is customer service-oriented and good at interacting with people, which are important qualities in managers.

- **Sales**: Most, if not all, technology companies that sell a product (hardware or software) have a sales department that is responsible for convincing people to buy that product. If you've had experience working with that product before and know exactly how it works and how to troubleshoot it, you can give potential customers details about how it can help them.

- **Consulting**: Consulting is typically short-term contracting. A consultant is hired to assist with hardware support and/or training for specific projects. Consultants are self-employed, which means they get to negotiate their pay rate, but it also means that work isn't guaranteed and can be erratic. Also, the hours can be outside of the normally scheduled workday, because consultants work around the schedules of others and the hiring company.

- **Technical writing**: Sometimes documentation is its own job, called a technical writer. Technical writers are responsible for translating technical language into something non-technical people can understand. They write the documentation that is released to the public, such as user's manuals and help sheets. Technical writing is challenging but rewarding, as it requires excellent communication skills and the ability to speak with both technical and non-technical people. In 2012, the median pay was $65,500 per year. Technical writing positions usually require a bachelor's degree, but it doesn't necessarily need to be a computer-related degree. English and communications degrees, for example, are valuable for the extensive amount of writing they require.

- **Network and systems administrators**: Network administrators know more and are responsible for more than network technicians. Systems administrators, or sys admins, as they're sometimes called, are responsible for a company's servers, the computers that run everything behind the scenes. In 2012, the median pay for both was $72,560 per year. Like consultants, network and sys admins can have strange hours, since they often need to work on the network and/or servers while no one else is using them. This is usually done late in the evening or on weekends. Most of these positions, even entry-level, will require a bachelor's in information technology or a related field.

- **Programmer**: There are many different types of programmers, who can work on anything from how a website looks (web designer) to building all types of software (software developer). Web designers typically focus on the user experience, i.e., how to make a website that looks attractive and is easy to navigate. So they need graphic design skills in addition to knowledge about programming. Web developers create programs that run websites behind the scenes, and software developers build other types of programs. The pay and hours can vary greatly between programmers, depending on their specialization and company for which they work. Many web designers, for example, are self-employed contractors. However, many programmers also work full time for specific companies. In 2012, the median income for a programmer was $74,280.

Tech support can be a career on its own, but it also gives you the tools to go in many different directions. A tech support employee's background in customer service means they have excellent communication skills, as well as a good idea of what customers want. There are even more options than those above, as you can use tech support as a jumping-off point to most other areas within IT. Specialize in something that you find interesting or useful, and that specialization will surely come in handy both within tech support and further down the road.

Tech support experience opens up a variety of career options.

Network techs are responsible for the physical components of a network.

Technical Support

3

ON THE JOB

S o now you know why tech support is so important, and what it takes to get a job in tech support. What might a typical day in tech support look like? Again, the answer to this varies, depending on the level of tech support you might be doing. We'll take a look at a variety of different possible tech support jobs, and what tasks they might do during a typical day.

There are three main categories of computer problems: software, hardware, and network. As a result, there are three main divisions of tech support. Each division works with the customer on different problems.

SOFTWARE TECH SUPPORT

There are many jobs that fall under software tech support, also called "desktop support," with many different job titles.

For example, entry-level desktop support employees often work in a help desk environment. They are responsible for receiving customer issues and logging them for other tech support employees to resolve. What sorts of things might a help desk technician deal with during a typical day?

HELP DESK TECHNICIAN

Help desk technicians are responsible for all incoming communication to a tech support department. This almost always involves talking on the phone, but can also involve any of the other methods of communication mentioned previously, such as walk-ins, e-mail, or even online chat. When customers contact the help desk, employees are responsible for taking down as much useful information as possible. This would include details such as the customer's name and contact information, as well as information about the issue and computer itself. This would include whether it's a Mac or PC, and what operating system it's running. Through asking other common types of questions, the tech will try to isolate whether this is the only computer or user experiencing this problem. For example, if it's a problem connecting to the Internet, or if the user can't print, is anyone else having the same issue? Another important question is how long the problem has occurred. Has it been happening for the last month, and has it gotten progressively worse? Or maybe it just started yesterday, after an unexpected power outage. The time period is important because it might allow tech support to figure out the catalyst for a problem. Why did it suddenly start happening now, or why did it suddenly get worse? Identifying trouble patterns is vital for figuring out what happened and how to resolve the issue.

The types of questions and issues a help desk technician will hear vary depending on where they work, of course. If they work at a tech company and help customers use their products, the questions will be specific to those products, like how to do something, or a feature that's not working correctly. If a tech

Help desk technicians often help customers over the phone as well as in person.

works at a consulting or another type of company, and offers general support to users, the questions could cover many topics.

With all of this information, a help desk technician will put in a ticket, or order, for someone to fix the problem. Large companies have database software that automatically assigns tickets to the person who needs to resolve the problem. The help desk technician is responsible for creating a ticket describing the problem in as much detail as possible. The more information a help desk technician can put in a ticket, the faster the next level of support can resolve the issue. This means help desk technicians are really important for making tech support departments run smoothly.

A help desk technician can fix some problems, if they're simple enough. This isn't commentary on how capable a help desk technician is at performing his or her job. Help desk technicians are very capable people. Rather, their responsibility is to spend their time performing intake and sending tickets to the correct people. So if a help desk technician has the time to fix a problem, or it won't tie up the phone line and prevent them from talking to other customers, they can sometimes troubleshoot a problem on their own. Companies often have limits—including time—on what sorts of questions help desk technicians can answer. Oftentimes they are provided a list of specific problems they can fix without putting in a ticket. The job of a help desk technician is reactive, meaning they spend most of the day waiting for customers to come to them with questions. They don't spend much time doing strategic long-term planning.

Although they're not required to fix the issue, help desk technicians are trained to perform basic troubleshooting. They will have the customer restart their computer or change their password or reset their wireless connection if it might help resolve the issue. "Have you tried turning it off and on again?" is a cliché users hear often, and for a reason. You'd be surprised how many issues that simple suggestion fixes.

After the basic questions, a help desk technician will try testing different parts of the issue. They'll ask more specific questions about the piece of technology having difficulties. If it's a problem with a website, for example, does the problem occur in all browsers? Strangely enough, no two browsers work the same. Many websites work best in one browser, and may not work at all in others. Testing the same website in a different browser can eliminate some potential causes.

If it's a common problem, the employee may have encountered it before and is familiar with the solution. If it's an uncommon problem, they'll need to do some research to find more information. Research can include looking up the issue in an internal knowledge base, asking another employee, or simply Googling the error message.

If it's more than a simple problem or cannot be easily resolved, the help desk technician is responsible for passing the ticket on to someone else in the department. This requires a good understanding of how the department works, and who is responsible for what types of problems. All of the details are recorded in the ticket so the next tech support employee knows what's happening and what's been tried so the process is as efficient as possible.

After the problem is resolved and the customer has been contacted, the employee who solved the issue will add the solution (and often their troubleshooting steps) to the ticket, and then mark it as "closed." That's it! If everything went smoothly, the problem has been fixed and the user is happy with his or her interactions.

Help desk technicians need to be able to multitask, and often have to jump quickly from issue to issue as they arise. Customers don't always have convenient timing, of course. Sometimes you end up with two people needing help at the same time. A good help desk technician has to be flexible and able to handle questions quickly and efficiently. If you like fast-paced environments, speaking directly to customers, and are interested in getting into tech support, help desk technicians and other similar positions are great starting points.

DESKTOP SUPPORT SPECIALIST

There are also upper-level desktop support positions that are responsible for troubleshooting more complicated questions. For example, after a help desk technician does preliminary troubleshooting and puts in a ticket, a desktop support specialist might receive that ticket and do more extensive research. Desktop support specialists are more experienced than help desk technicians, so they answer more complicated problems. Desktop support specialists can also be responsible for answering customers' "how-to" questions in addition to troubleshooting problems. Here are some examples of how-to questions in common applications:

- How do I add another e-mail account to a desktop e-mail application such as Microsoft Outlook or Apple Mail?

- How do I add superscript to my toolbar in Microsoft Word?

- How can I connect a Bluetooth device (such as a mouse, keyboard, or speakers) to my computer or mobile device?

These examples are fairly simple how-to questions, and help desk technicians may also be able to answer them. The line between what a help desk technician and a desktop support specialist can and should do is fuzzy, and varies from company to company. Sometimes desktop support employees specialize in different types of software, and are regarded as the expert for that software. As a result, they'll receive any questions related to that software that are beyond the basics.

In some companies, customers and/or employees can sign up for training classes on the uses of different software. Desktop support specialists are the ones who teach these training classes. Training is basically a longer answer to a how-to question, which is why the same people often do both. A desktop support specialist, for example, might be responsible for teaching classes or designing other training materials like help sheets. What sorts of questions fall into this in-depth training category? A customer might want to learn how to make **macros** in Excel, which are snapshots of a specific, repetitive process, an example being a spreadsheet containing a process that has to be repeated with some regularity. Macros are immensely useful but are a more advanced tool of Excel. As a result, entry-level help desk technicians aren't required to know how to make and use them.

Desktop support specialists can also be trained on less common software. There are many applications that have specialized uses. While a help desk technician can answer questions about common software like Microsoft Office, they may need to transfer questions immediately if they involve something more complicated, like SPSS (statistics software) or FileMaker Pro (database software). Desktop support specialists have more experience in more areas. People who have a level of expertise with specific programs are often tier three of tech support, where they're allowed to be more strategic about the help they give customers. Tier three desktop support employees have the time and resources to provide formal, in-depth training

Desktop support specialists often provide training to users.

to their clients. Desktop support is a great place to be if you like teaching people new things.

Instead of becoming an expert in specific software, some desktop support specialists will specialize in company policy. This means that a desktop support specialist can be trained to deal with internal matters like legal practices, or have the authority to settle billing disputes. If a company makes software, there will also be support specialists who work closely with the programmers to fix bugs. The support specialist will keep track of what bugs customers encounter, and how common they are. Then they'll work alongside programmers to fix the bugs. Help desk technicians and other tier-one tech support positions allow you to dabble and learn a little about everything. When you have the experience, second- and third-tier positions, such as desktop support specialists, give you the freedom to specialize in a topic and learn as much about it as you can. It's a lot of fun to get to this point and be regarded as the expert.

Why Do Browsers Work Differently?

Browsers automatically read HTML, CSS, and JavaScript, and display what the site tells them to display. A program called a **rendering engine**, also called a layout engine, is used to do this. Every major browser (Safari, Internet Explorer, Chrome, and Firefox) uses a different rendering engine, so they all read a website's code differently. Good web designers account for this by adding extra rules to websites, such as, "If you're running a version of Internet Explorer older than _, do this instead." This doesn't always happen, though. Adding exceptions for all browsers is time-consuming and complicated. It also means you have to be able to test the site in all those browsers to see what looks out of place. Web designers don't always have the spare time and resources to do this.

There are often cosmetic differences in how a website is viewed in different browsers, and sometimes there are larger functional differences as well. For example, the Mac version of Chrome doesn't currently support Java (a common web programming language), and Flash (software from Adobe that runs interactive videos and games) doesn't work on Safari on iOS devices.

There are also differences between browsers that are due to user settings. A user's default browser, the one they use most of the time, stores information in **cookies** and the **cache**, and has add-ons installed by the user. Cookies are small pieces of data stored on your computer by different websites that help those websites remember your computer. This is how individual sites remember all of your settings and whether or not you're logged into an account. Your browser's cache keeps snapshots of all the websites you visit frequently, so that it can load them quickly when you visit that specific site again. Sometimes a website is updated, though. You then have to clear the cache to view the newest version of the site. Using a different browser is like having a clean slate because those cookies and the cache do not sync across browsers.

As you can see, there are a lot of reasons a website could be behaving weirdly in a particular browser. Trying another browser is a great way to figure out if an issue is only happening in a specific browser, which is why it's a common troubleshooting step. It gets you one step closer to fixing the issue.

HARDWARE TECHNICIAN

There are a couple of types of hardware technicians. First, we'll look at in-house hardware techs. These people work on computers at the company rather than going to the customer. Then we'll look at field techs, who go out into the field and fix computers on-location. There's a lot of overlap between the two categories, so we'll compare and contrast.

IN-HOUSE HARDWARE TECHNICIANS

Some companies offer hardware support but don't travel to the customer's home or office. Most computer repair stores fall into this category, as do brand-specific hardware companies, such as Dell and Apple. A hardware tech will set up faulty computers at their tech bench and run tests and replace parts as needed.

Hardware techs aren't usually the first people consulted about an issue, so other tech support employees will notify them when there's a problem they need to fix. First-tier tech support, such as help desk technicians, will receive issues and put a ticket in the hardware techs' queue. A queue is basically a to-do list of all the issues they need to resolve, and the time in which all work should be completed. Sometimes the computer will be brought to them, and sometimes they'll go to the computer and run tests, then bring it back to their tech bench. What sorts of hardware problems might a tech test for and fix? A common problem is hard drive failure. There are a lot of ways a hard drive can break. Hard drives have spinning parts that wear down over time. Since their parts move, dropping a hard drive can break those parts. Large magnets can also damage hard drives, because they use electromagnetic currents to move and store information. Hard drives have a lifespan of about three to five years, and when they fail, they just need to be replaced.

Most any other piece of hardware can be replaced individually, from the display to the battery to the RAM. Not all of them are worth the effort, though, as batteries are often glued in place, and replacing **motherboards** (also called logic boards) can be almost

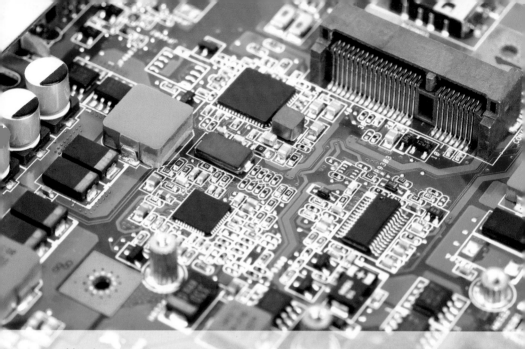

Hardware techs test computers and replace broken components.

as expensive as buying a new computer. If your computer is still under warranty, the manufacturer will replace parts for free, as long as you did not cause the damages by doing something such as dropping the unit or spilling water on its keyboard. Hardware techs have the ability to look up your computer by its serial number. This tells them how old it is, what parts they can replace for free, and the items or services for which they will charge.

In order to change out hardware, techs are usually required to have hardware certificates from the manufacturer. A hardware tech will be certified by Dell, Lenovo, Apple, or another company if they need to repair those types of computers. Although computers often look similar on the surface, they have vastly different parts inside, so it's important for hardware techs to be familiar with the brands they troubleshoot. Each manufacturer supplies their certified techs with hardware tests. Hardware tests are usually automated programs that test individual parts one at a time, such as the battery, the hard drive, and the RAM. The test will note parts that are failing, so the tech knows what to replace.

Hardware techs work with their hands a lot, moving around tiny computer parts and even tinier screws. As a result, they require good fine-motor skills and a lot of patience. If you like exploring the inner parts of a computer and seeing how they all work together, hardware support would be a great way to go. Hardware techs often stay at their benches, so they don't interact directly with customers as much as other tech support roles.

FIELD TECHNICIANS

Some hardware techs are called field techs, because they go out into the field and fix problems on location. Field techs are a

The Geek Squad field technicians will visit customers' homes to fix computer problems.

subset of hardware techs. The big difference is that field techs often do more than fix hardware. If a hardware tech is a field tech, they often give training to customers. Field techs can act as consultants, answering customers' "how-to" questions in addition to resolving issues. Field techs often work for third-party consulting companies like the Geek Squad.

Resolving an issue can range from changing a setting to reinstalling some software or even the entire operating system, to replacing a bad piece of hardware. There's some overlap with desktop support here, obviously. If a field tech works for a small company, they're much more likely to do training in addition to repairing issues, since employees at small companies must wear many hats to support their users' needs.

What might a field tech's day look like? Like other second-tier hardware and software support positions, field techs have a queue, a sequence of messages or jobs. They'll be notified (by e-mail, phone, or in person) when there's a new issue in the queue. The first tier of tech support tries to gather as much information as possible, but it's not always enough to solve the problem without seeing the computer. Field techs can fill in the gaps by diagnosing those computers onsite. It's much easier to see what program is displaying the error message, or to quickly change a setting, for example, when you're standing right next to the computer. Being there and able to walk people through things is much simpler than being on the phone with them. This is especially valuable with less technically savvy customers, because you can see exactly what they're trying to do. When the issue is resolved, a field tech may train the customer on another related issue. For example, if the issue was installing a new printer, the field tech could then walk the customer through printing to that specific printer. The field tech will then close the ticket and move on to the next issue in their queue.

Field techs train customers much like the tier two desktop support team. They provide informal training that doesn't take very long, as opposed to planned, formal classes and help sheets. The questions are usually simple, such as those listed in the sample how-to questions in the desktop support specialist section. The field tech's primary responsibility is making sure everything works properly, and that the customer can successfully use the computer for basic tasks like word processing and browsing the Internet.

Field techs can often work for independent computer consulting companies. A consulting company is a small business that provides third-party tech support for a fee. Consulting companies are often owned and managed by people who were in tech support before they became managers. Field techs in this sort of job have to be adaptable, as they'll encounter all types of computers and software that exist. Field techs who work as consultants can also be contractors, meaning they're self-employed and set their own wages and hours.

Field techs are the jacks-of-all-trades in tech support. They know a little bit of everything. They have to know hardware, because they're often onsite without anyone else around to ask. They have to know software. They also need great customer service skills, self-sufficiency, and the confidence to work alone most of the time.

NETWORK TECHNICIAN

Network technicians are responsible for all the bits and pieces of a network, including its hardware and software. Their job is to understand and maintain the network architecture, which means knowing how all the pieces of a network talk to each other. Large companies will need at least one dedicated network technician, because the company's network is so large and complicated. Network technicians can also work for smaller companies, or sometimes they work on a contractual, or freelance, basis. For small businesses, it's not worth having a full- or even part-time network tech on hand, so there are network techs that work as contractors and serve many small businesses.

The network itself can be an Ethernet (wired) network or a wireless network. This is network hardware, and many companies have both types of networks. Ethernet and wireless networks come with their own challenges. Ethernet networks require the installation of the Ethernet wires and the boxes that connect them all together. At a large company, there's even more to think about. Here, the wires are hidden in the walls and are accessed via Ethernet ports that are embedded in the walls. Large networks also include huge hubs stored in network closets where many Ethernet connections come together, linking all of the local computers with the rest of the Internet.

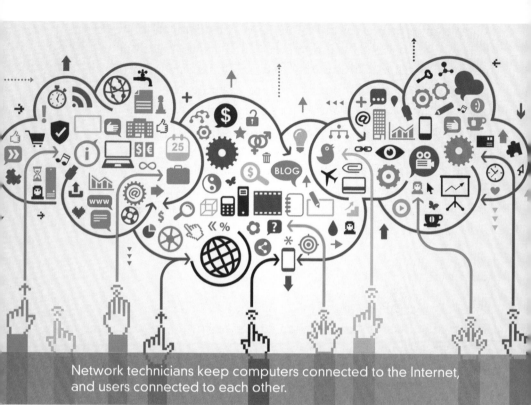

Network technicians keep computers connected to the Internet, and users connected to each other.

With wireless networks, on the other hand, network techs have to consider signal strength and the different types of wireless signals they can use in a network. Wireless **routers** (the device that does the actual work of broadcasting the wireless signal) can interfere with each other, as can furniture and walls. Network techs take all of these things into account when building networks.

Large networks include servers, or specialized computers that provide information to people through the Internet. There are many types of servers that have different functions. For example, anything that you access through the Internet is on a server somewhere, including websites, online games, databases, and file storage. Network techs aren't directly responsible for servers, as that's the job of systems administrators, but they do make sure that people can access them through the network.

Since so many pieces go into making a physical network, network techs use specialized software to monitor its

performance. The software create an alarm when something is struggling, such as if too many people are connecting in one area and the network can't support them all, or if any equipment has failed. They can also use software to remotely control the network, such as turning off unused Ethernet ports.

Being a network tech is like being a field tech in some ways, because network techs spend a lot of time in the field, adjusting the physical parts of the network. Network techs rarely interact directly with customers, though, and they're not responsible for training

Technical Support

users. Network techs need to be independent and comfortable working alone. If you're less interested in talking with customers and helping them directly, this could be a good direction. Network techs also have to be interested in networks, obviously. This is a great path for someone who wants to know exactly how computers talk to each other. It's a complicated and interesting process, and always provides new challenges.

No matter what direction you want to go within tech support, all tech support employees enjoy knowing how technology works and tinkering with computers. From there, they specialize depending on their interests. If you really enjoy talking to customers and solving problems with them, you'll probably want to do something in desktop and front-end support. If you like working alone and resolving hardware issues, consider hardware and network support.

WHERE DO YOU WANT TO WORK?

Computers have become so important in daily life that all companies use them, including places that don't have a specific technology focus—like grocery stores. Since computers are so heavily used, all companies rely on tech support in some way, whether it's having their own IT departments or hiring contractors for tech support when they need it. This is great for you because it means you can work in a variety of places. Keep in

Non-technical companies often rely on computers to run point-of-sales (POS) systems and do bookkeeping.

mind that the daily ins and outs of a tech support job varies a lot depending on the company for which you work.

For example, working as a contractor or for a small consulting company is very different than working for a large corporation. Consultants spend most of their time moving from one location to another, serving clients that don't need a dedicated full-time staff person. They do a lot of the same work in multiple locations, such as setting up and maintaining small computer networks and setting up printers or installing software. Individual consultants can work as contractors on projects. Contractors like this generally have specific skills, so they work for a company to help implement a short-term project then move on to help another company. They're self-employed, so contractors negotiate their own wages and hours.

Another possible option is working for a nonprofit. Nonprofits always pay less than for-profit companies. They simply don't have the funding to pay as well. However, this is often balanced by an informal work environment and dedicated, enthusiastic workforce. Chapter 4 will get more into salary and benefits comparisons. For now, keep in mind that there are a variety of work environments, and that different environments will have different day-to-day job responsibilities as well as different salaries and benefits.

One of the biggest categorizations is the company's product. If a company's primary product is technology, whether it's software or hardware, it provides a very different environment than working at a company that offers other products and services. The difference in product also makes a difference in company culture, especially in how you as a tech support employee interact with the rest of the employees. For instance, at a tech company, the majority of employees are technical, whether they're in support or development. On the other hand, at non-technical companies, the majority of employees aren't technical, making you the only tech support contact helping them. The dynamic is different when you're supporting internal employees, because you repeatedly interact with the same people. You're able to build long-term relationships with them. Knowing your clients means you know how computer-savvy they are, which helps you speed up your troubleshooting. At tech companies where you're providing external tech support, however, you'll constantly interact with different people. Neither situation is better or worse, but it is something to consider when thinking about where you want to work.

There are a variety of factors you should think about when comparing jobs.

Technical Support

4

SALARY AND BENEFITS

L et's get down to the details of what salary and benefits you can expect from a career in tech support. There was a bit about this at the end of Chapter 2, but now it's time to get specific.

SALARY

As you read in the last chapter, there are several jobs that fall within tech support. Likewise, their salaries vary. What can you expect to earn in the field of tech support? According to the *Occupational Outlook Handbook (OOH)*, published by the United States Department of Labor, desktop support employees earned a median of $46,420 in 2012. This number is a bit confusing because it includes both entry-level desktop support positions, such as help desk technicians, and more experienced positions, such as desktop support specialists. The *OOH* helps by dividing this group by percentile: "the lowest 10 percent earned less than $27,620, and the top 10 percent earned more than $77,430." This gives you a good idea of how income varies according to experience and the company for which you work.

What about hardware support and network techs? Although the *OOH* doesn't have any specific data for hardware techs and field techs, it does have data for network support specialists, who are a type of network tech. Network techs and hardware techs earn comparable wages. Network support specialists had a median income of $59,090 in 2012. Network techs earn higher wages than employees in desktop support because the position requires more experience in entry-level positions and more in-depth technical knowledge for upper-level positions. The starting salary for an entry-level network or hardware tech is higher than that of a help desk technician. Upper-level hardware and network techs likewise have higher incomes. According to the *OOH*, the top 10 percent of network support specialists make more than $96,850.

If you want to use tech support as a stepping-stone to other areas of IT, you have a lot of options, as you discovered at the end of Chapter 2. How do those compare to the above-mentioned incomes? Network admins, a step above network techs in experience and responsibilities, have a median income of $72,560. Keep in mind that the step from network tech to network admin requires more than work experience. Network admin positions will often require a college degree, whereas network tech positions don't. Network tech to network admin is the most direct path from tech support to other IT positions, but there are many other paths you can take.

There's obviously a lot of variance in those salaries. What factors might go into a higher or lower salary? A big part of determining any salary is cost of living. The same job in large cities with higher costs of living, such as New York City, Boston, or San Francisco, will pay more than it would in other places. Large cities are more expensive, as housing, food, and shopping all cost more. Salaries take this into account. If you are curious about the

Your salary will depend on what type of tech support you do and the company for which you work.

cost of living in a specific location, there are several great tools to help you. These include CNN's cost of living calculator: money.cnn.com/calculator/pf/cost-of-living.

Of course, salaries also vary depending on the experience level required and the job's specialization. As you have already read, entry-level help desk technicians won't make as much as higher-level positions. This is standard for most industries. There's also smaller incremental differences between someone who's been working in a job for six months versus someone who's been working the same job for two to three years. Higher education also counts as experience. People with degrees tend to make more than those without them. More experienced positions also tend to be more specialized, which means there is more demand for an individual's skills. A greater demand equals greater pay. Demand for a job can be driven by many factors. For example, if a company really needs someone to fill a specific position, they're often willing to pay more. Jobs also have market values, which is an average wage employees receive for their skill sets. Employees can negotiate their wages with their employers if they feel they are underpaid. However, if you are in an entry-level position, it is unlikely that you will be offered an increase in salary until you have been at the company at least more than one year.

The company's size also impacts the salary. Someone working for a large corporation, for example, will make more money than someone working for a nonprofit. If you find a job you're interested in, do research on both the company and the job itself. Find out the market value for the job and what you can expect from the company in benefits, which may balance out a lower salary. You don't have to make your decision based solely on salary, either. If you think one company is a better fit and that you'll be more fulfilled there, you can make your own decision about how important salary is to you.

BENEFITS

Unless you're working as an independent, self-employed contractor, you'll certainly receive benefits, such as health insurance, vacation time, and sick leave. Companies offer an average of nine paid holidays in addition to vacation time and sick leave. The holidays are typically days such as Memorial Day or Thanksgiving. Typically you don't have to work on these days and will be paid without having to use your personal vacation or sick time. The amounts of each benefit will vary greatly depending on where you work.

Health insurance is complicated, but there are many tools available to help you wade through your options. Larger companies will provide options for you to choose from, and there will be employees available for you to consult about selecting the one best for you. Dental and vision coverage is sometimes, but not always, included in health benefits.

Employee Benefits Package

Common benefits include health care, vacation time, and sick days.

There are two ways you pay for health insurance: the premium, which is how much you pay each payroll period, and the out-of-pocket expenses, which is what you pay per doctor's visit. Typically, a regular doctor's check-up is free, and your health insurance will have a detailed breakdown of how much you'll pay for other services. As the premium increases, your out-of-pocket expenses become lower.

What types of features should you look for in vacation time and sick leave? Of course, you'll want to look at how fast these days accumulate over time. Usually you'll receive a set amount of new vacation and sick time each pay period. Not all companies allow vacation and sick time to roll over to the next year, which is called a "use it or lose it" policy. Most of the time, companies don't have a deliberate "use it or lose it" policy, but instead allow some portion of sick and vacation time to roll over rather than the entire amount. Companies will usually pay out any unused vacation time when you leave, but not unused sick time.

Some companies combine vacation time and sick leave into one general category called paid time off (PTO), which has pros and cons. PTO tends to accumulate faster than separate vacation and sick time, but slower than both categories combined. It also makes people less likely to take sick days, since taking sick time happens at the expense of vacations and other personal time off. Just keep in mind that this is another example of how benefits work.

There are other common benefits as well, such as a retirement portfolio. A retirement portfolio is a collection of investments that are managed for you. All you have to do is contribute a percentage of your paycheck every pay period. Employers often contribute to their employees' retirement funds, although the amount they contribute varies. This probably isn't something you think about much right now, but it's invaluable later in life.

PERKS

Every day the world becomes more and more connected by technological advances. Now more than ever, the tech industry is booming and tech jobs are in high demand. As a result, companies are trying to find new ways to attract employees to work for them. This often involves offering advantages to working at the company. Depending on the company, perks can include anything from being allowed to bring your dog to work, to tuition assistance if you want to pursue higher education. Some companies have transportation assistance, such as subsidized public transportation passes or perks for employees who choose to bike to work. Fitness benefits, such as an onsite gym, or discounted rates for a local fitness center, are common.

If you work in the tech industry, the job perks usually include technology. There's almost always an employee discount on company products as well. If you work for Microsoft or Apple, for example, you can buy their products at a discount. Most companies provide individual computers for employees to use, and some

Companies in Silicon Valley provide shuttle buses for employees living in San Francisco.

companies allow their employees to choose their computers or laptops so they can work from anywhere. Dropbox takes it a step further, giving its employees the option to build their own company computers.

Large tech companies, such as Google, have extensive employee benefits in order to attract and retain employees. Since companies use these offerings to encourage people to work for them, they're usually posted on company websites. On Google's website, for example, these benefits include travel insurance, paid maternity and paternity leave, and reimbursement for taking college and training classes. They also include fun activities, such as workshops, where people can, in their free time, learn how to create electronic devices. Employees can also eat whatever they want from the office pantries, which are constantly stocked.

Corporate culture can be an important factor in deciding where you want to work.

Then there are more subtle and qualitative perks. A company's work environment isn't strictly a perk, but it's definitely something you should pay attention to. Some companies have more formal work environments than others. As with everything else, this varies from company to company, although there are some general rules. Banks and other large for-profit corporations tend to be formal, while educational work environments, such as colleges, nonprofits, and small companies, tend to be more informal. This difference manifests in a variety of ways. Large for-profit companies typically have stricter dress codes, for example, and may require employees to dress in formal office clothing, such as skirts or slacks, or even suits. This is a place where salary is balanced by other benefits, where the higher the salary, the stricter the dress code is. The formality of the work environment tends to increase with the size of the company. This isn't always true, but it's a good rule of thumb to pay attention to when you're looking for jobs.

EXPLORING CORPORATE CULTURE

Another important aspect of a job is corporate culture, the combining of the values, beliefs, taboos, symbols, rituals, and myths all companies develop over time. What makes a culture is the blend of employees and environment. Each culture is unique and many factors go into creating one. How do you recognize a great fit for you?

Great culture starts with a vision or mission statement, or simple phrases that guide a company's values and provide it with purpose. For example, Microsoft's mission is to "enable people and businesses throughout the world to realize their full potential."

A company's values are the core of its culture. While a vision expresses the company's purpose, values offer a set of guidelines on the behaviors needed to achieve that vision. Google's values

"   "

It's important that the company be a family, that people feel that they're part of the company, and that the company is like a family to them. When you treat people that way, you get better productivity.

LARRY PAGE, CO-FOUNDER AND CEO OF GOOGLE, INC., ON WHY GOOGLE HAS SO MANY PERKS might be best articulated by its famous slogan, "Don't be evil." They also hold fast to their "ten things we know to be true." While many companies find their values revolve around a few simple topics, employees, clients, professionalism, the originality of those values is less important than their authenticity.

There are other factors that influence culture. Identifying and understanding them more fully in an existing organization can be the first step to knowing how comfortable you will be in the workplace.

PREPARING FOR THE JOB

There are a lot of details to consider if you want to work in tech support. First, develop a timeline of where you want to be after high school. Do you want to consider going to college, or try to gain experience on your own by going into a customer service job or taking on an internship? Next, figure out what type of technology career you would be good at and enjoy doing. It all depends on what you're interested in and how your personality and skills match the specific career. You don't have to have all of the answers now, but you should consider these points if you are serious about a career in technology.

Before you decide what area you want to specialize in, take some time to reflect:

- What is your personality like, and where do you think you would do best?

- What are you already good at, and what areas are you interested in improving?

- Would you rather work with customers or work behind the scenes?

- What type of work environment interests you?

- What are your goals? What do you want out of your career?

You can start preparing now for whatever career you choose.

Tech support requires many of the same skills highly prized in other types of jobs, such as good communication and customer service skills. It also requires some fairly unique skills, such as constantly challenging yourself to learn new technologies. The tech industry in general is fast-paced as new technologies come and go quickly. Thus to keep pace, those in tech support must stay up to date on new products and software. If you're interested in technology and the tech industry but don't know where to start, tech support will allow you to gain experience and learn about different areas within the field.

If you've read this book and are still interested in tech support as a career, what next? There's nothing to stop you from tinkering with computers now instead of later. Try finding information about how computers work and how to get a job in the tech industry, such as the resources provided at the end of this book. Find other people who work in the tech industry and ask them lots of questions about what their jobs are like. Try to gain work and volunteer experience related to what you want to do. Explore colleges that offer technology degrees you're interested in earning. Plan and prepare. Any experience is good experience when getting your first job.

Remember that the tech industry is incredibly diverse. If you like working with computers, there's a place for you. No matter your career path, find something that makes you happy and that you can see yourself doing for a long time. Good luck in whatever career you choose!

GLOSSARY

algorithm Step-by-step instructions for the computer on how to perform a task.

analog A device that reads and calculates a continuous curve of data. This is in contrast to digital devices, which read and store data through a collection of on/off switches that are symbolized as ones and zeros.

binary The basic language of all digital computers, in which information is either coded as a one (on) or a zero (off).

browser A specific type of computer program that allows a user to access and surf the Internet. Internet Explorer, Firefox, and Chrome are all examples of common browsers.

bug A flaw in a piece of software that makes the software behave strangely and/or return an incorrect result.

cache Your browser's cache keeps snapshots of all the sites you visit frequently, so that it can load them quickly when you revisit the site.

certification An award that indicates a level of competence in a specific skill. Certifications are gained by passing a test, and there are many different types for different skills.

cookie A piece of information stored on your computer that tells a website who you are. This is how websites remember that you're logged in, and allow you to stay logged in.

GLOSSARY

documentation Instructions on how to use and troubleshoot a product. Examples of documentation can include user manuals, internal knowledge bases, and help menus.

floppy disk A floppy disk is an old type of external storage that held very limited amounts of space. Floppy disks, like other external storage, such as CDs and external hard drives, were used for saving files and making backups.

hardware The physical parts that make up a piece of technology. Typically used to refer to the physical parts of a computer (e.g., monitor, mouse, hard drive, processor, etc.).

knowledge base An internal database full of questions and solutions, used by tech support employees to answer customers' questions.

macro A list of steps recorded by the user to transform input into a specific type of output. Macros are often used to automate repetitive calculations in Excel and other data-related software, such as statistics programs.

modular Something that can be broken down into smaller parts and easily reused in other projects. Both hardware and software can be modular.

motherboard Also called a logic board, the motherboard holds all of the tiny circuits and processors that perform all of the computer's thinking.

Technical Support

network A group of computers that can communicate with each other, as well as the technology that allows that communication (e.g., wireless, Ethernet, etc.).

rendering engine Also called a layout engine, a rendering engine is the part of a browser that actually takes the code of a website and translates it into the graphics, layout, and text that we see when we go to that page. Browsers use different rendering engines, which is why web pages can look different when viewed in different browsers.

router Part of a wireless network, a router is the device that does the actual work of broadcasting the wireless signal.

server A computer that provides information to another computer. There are many types of servers that provide different types of information, such as hosting websites or games, so that other computers can access them over the Internet.

software Programs that allow a computer to do something specific. Examples include: word processor, photo-editing, and operating system software.

SOURCE NOTES

INTRODUCTION

(1) p. 9: Hansen, Drew. "Myth Busted: Steve Jobs Did Listen to Customers," *Forbes*, December 19, 2013. www.forbes. com/sites/drewhansen/2013/12/19/myth-busted-steve-jobs-did-listen-to-customers.

CHAPTER 1

(1) p. 13: "Personal Computers Exhibition," Computer History Museum. Accessed April 16, 2014. www.computerhistory.org/revolution/personal-computers/17/296.

(2) p. 13: "Personal Computers Exhibition," Computer History Museum.

(3) p. 14: Corn, Joseph J. User Unfriendly: Consumer Struggles with Personal Technologies, from Clocks and Sewing Machines to Cars and Computers (Baltimore, Maryland: The Johns Hopkins University Press, 2011), p. 198.

(4) p. 15: Gallo, Carmine. "Apple's Secret Employee Training Manual Reinvents Customer Service in Seven Ways," *Forbes*, August 30, 2012. Accessed April 18, 2014. www.forbes.com/sites/carminegallo/2012/08/30/apples-secret-employee-training-manual-reinvents-customer-service-in-seven-ways.

(5) p. 16: Corn, Joseph J. User Unfriendly, p. 197.

(6) p. 21: "Personal Computers Exhibition," Computer History Museum.

(7) p. 20: Mike Maples, interview by Larry Welke, May 6, 2004. "PC Software Workshop: Technical—Customer Support," Needham, Massachusetts. archive.computerhistory. org/resources/text/Oral_History/PC_Software/Technical_ Customer_Support.oral_history.2004.102702029.pdf.

(8) p. 21: Maleshefski, Tiffany. "The History of Customer Support," Zendesk. Accessed April 17, 2014. www.zendesk. com/blog/the-history-of-customer-support.

(9) p. 22: Maples, "PC Software Workshop: Technical—Customer Support."

CHAPTER 2

(1) p. 37: Weese, Ashley. "Customer Service: Then and Now." www.youtube.com/watch?v=4byuQsrsiHU.

(2) p. 43: Maples, "PC Software Workshop: Technical—Customer Support."

(3) p. 45: "Technical Writers," *Occupational Outlook Handbook*. Accessed April 18, 2014. www.bls.gov/ooh/media-and-communication/technical-writers.htm.

SOURCE NOTES

(4) p. 45: "Network and Computer Systems Administrators," *Occupational Outlook Handbook*. Accessed April 18, 2014. www.bls.gov/ooh/computer-and-information-technology/ network-and-computer-systems-administrators.htm.

(5) p. 46: "Computer Programmers," *Occupational Outlook Handbook*, accessed May 6, 2014. www.bls.gov/ooh/computer-and-information-technology/computer-programmers.htm.

CHAPTER 4

(1) p. 70: "Computer Support Specialists," *Occupational Outlook Handbook*. Accessed May 5, 2014. www.bls.gov/ooh/ computer-and-information-technology/computer-support-specialists.htm.

(2) p. 70: "Computer Support Specialists," *Occupational Outlook Handbook*.

(3) p. 70: "Network and Computer Systems Administrators," *Occupational Outlook Handbook*. Accessed May 5, 2014. www.bls.gov/ooh/computer-and-information-technology/ network-and-computer-systems-administrators.htm.

(4) p. 72: "Paid Time Off Programs and Practices," WorldatWork, May 2010. Accessed May 18, 2014. www.worldatwork.org/ waw/adimLink?id=38913.

(5) p. 74: "Paid Time Off Programs and Practices," WorldatWork.

(6) p. 75: Lynley, Matt. "20 Reasons You Wish You Worked At A Tech Company," *Business Insider*, July 30, 2012. www.businessinsider.com/the-best-perks-in-tech-2012-7?op=1.

(7) p. 75: "Benefits - Google Careers," Google. Accessed May 18, 2014. www.google.com/about/careers/lifeatgoogle/benefits.

(8) p. 75: Stanger, Melissa. "18 of the Best Perks at Top Employers," *Business Insider*, February 11, 2013, accessed May 18, 2014. www.businessinsider.com/companies-with-awesome-perks-payscale-2013-1?op=1.

(9) p. 77: Larry Page, interview by Adam Lashinsky, January 19, 2012, "Larry Page: Google should be like a family." tech.fortune.cnn.com/2012/01/19/best-companies-google-larry-page/?iid=F_F500M.

FURTHER INFORMATION

BOOKS

Alpern, Naomi J., Joey Alpern, and Randy Muller. *IT Career JumpStart: An Introduction to PC Hardware, Software, and Networking*. New York, NY: Wiley, 2012.

Farr, Michael. *Top 100 Computer and Technical Careers: Your Complete Guidebook to Major Jobs in Many Fields at All Training Levels*. 4th ed. Indianapolis, IN: JIST Publishing, 2009.

Fogg, Neeta. *College Majors Handbook with Real Career Paths and Payoffs: The Actual Jobs, Earnings, and Trends for Graduates of 50 College Majors*. 3rd ed. St. Paul, MN: Jist Works, 2012.

Franek, Robert, Kristen O'Toole, and David Soto. *The Best 378 Colleges: 2014 Edition*. Framingham, MA: The Princeton Review, 2013.

Moran, Matthew. *Building Your IT Career: A Complete Toolkit for a Dynamic Career in Any Economy*. 2nd ed. Indianapolis, IN: Pearson IT Certification, 2013.

WEBSITES

College Board Major and Career Search

www.bigfuture.collegeboard.org/majors-careers

The College Board has the most comprehensive list of possible majors, as well as information on a variety of IT careers. They have reflective questions about your interests and personality, as well as practical information like tips on how to plan for a career in high school and what salary you can expect in certain careers.

Khan Academy

www.khanacademy.org

Khan Academy is like a MOOC (see below) in that you can watch educational videos then take quizzes and do exercises to test your knowledge. The tutorials are designed by a small team of people not affiliated with any college, unlike other MOOC websites. Khan Academy has a variety of courses, including a few on computer science and more on computer programming.

MOOCs

www.udacity.com, www.coursera.org, www.edx.org

Udacity, Coursera, and edX all provide MOOCs that you can access online for free. Classes vary greatly on an individual scale, so feel free to browse both within an individual website and between the three.

FURTHER INFORMATION

Occupational Outlook Handbook

www.bls.gov/ooh

Maintained by the United States Department of Labor, the *Occupational Outlook Handbook* is a great resource for any job or career you might be thinking about. It provides detailed information about how to prepare for a given career, what the job responsibilities will be, and what the salaries and benefits are like.

Stack Exchange

stackexchange.com/sites

Stack Exchange is a collection of websites, where people ask questions about a variety of topics, and experts answer them. Anyone can ask a question, and people vote for the best answers. Stack Overflow (stackoverflow.com) is the largest community, and programmers use it regularly. But there are other communities too! If you're curious about computer science (cs.stackexchange. com) or network engineering (networkengineering. stackexchange.com), you can browse their respective websites to get a feel for what people do in these fields.

Unigo

www.unigo.com

A college review website, Unigo sets itself apart by the amount of information contributed by current students. There are reviews, ratings, photos, and videos all from students who attend the colleges being reviewed.

BIBLIOGRAPHY

"Benefits - Google Careers," Google. Accessed May 18, 2014. www.google.com/about/careers/lifeatgoogle/benefits.

Computer History Museum. "Personal Computers Exhibition." Accessed April 16, 2014. www.computerhistory.org/revolution/personal-computers/17/296.

Corn, Joseph J. *User Unfriendly: Consumer Struggles with Personal Technologies, from Clocks and Sewing Machines to Cars and Computers*. Baltimore, MD: The Johns Hopkins University Press, 2011.

Da Cruz, Frank. "The IBM 610 Auto-Point Computer." Columbia University, updated October 22, 2013. Accessed April 18, 2014. www.columbia.edu/cu/computinghistory/610.html.

Drummer, G. W. A. *Electronic Inventions and Discoveries: Electronics from its earliest beginnings to the present day*. Bristol, UK: Institute of Physics Publishing, 1997.

Farr, Michael. *Top 100 Computer and Technical Careers: Your Complete Guidebook to Major Jobs in Many Fields at All Training Levels*. Indianapolis, IN: JIST Publishing, 2009.

Gallo, Carmine. "Apple's Secret Employee Training Manual Reinvents Customer Service in Seven Ways," *Forbes*, August 30, 2012. Accessed April 18, 2014. www.forbes.com/sites/carminegallo/2012/08/30/apples-secret-employee-training-manual-reinvents-customer-service-in-seven-ways.

BIBLIOGRAPHY

Hansen, Drew. "Myth Busted: Steve Jobs Did Listen to Customers," *Forbes*, December 19, 2013. www.forbes.com/sites/drewhansen/2013/12/19/myth-busted-steve-jobs-did-listen-to-customers.

Larry Page, interview by Adam Lashinsky, January 19, 2012, "Larry Page: Google should be like a family." tech.fortune.cnn.com/2012/01/19/best-companies-google-larry-page/?iid=F_F500M.

Lynley, Matt. "20 Reasons You Wish You Worked At A Tech Company," *Business Insider*, July 30, 2012. www.businessinsider.com/the-best-perks-in-tech-2012-7?op=1.

Maleshefski, Tiffany. "The History of Customer Support," Zendesk. Accessed April 17, 2014. www.zendesk.com/blog/the-history-of-customer-support.

Mike Maples, interview by Larry Welke, May 6, 2004, "PC Software Workshop: Technical - Customer Support," Needham, MA. http://archive.computerhistory.org/resources/text/Oral_History/PC_Software/Technical_Customer_Support.oral_history.2004.102702029.pdf.

"Paid Time Off Programs and Practices," WorldatWork, May 2010. Accessed May 18, 2014. www.worldatwork.org/waw/adimLink?id=38913.

Rich, Jason. *202 High-Paying Jobs You Can Land Without a College Degree*. Irvine, CA: Entrepreneur Press, 2006.

Stanger, Melissa. "18 of the Best Perks at Top Employers," *Business Insider*, February 11, 2013, accessed May 18, 2014, www.businessinsider.com/companies-with-awesome-perks-payscale-2013-1?op=1.

United States Bureau of Labor. "Occupational Outlook Handbook." Last modified January 8, 2014. www.bls.gov/ooh.

Weese, Ashley. "Customer Service: Then and Now." SIGUCCS Conference, March 11 2014. www.youtube.com/watch?v=4byuQsrsiHU.

INDEX

Page numbers in **boldface** are illustrations.

ABOUT THE AUTHOR

RACHEL KING has worked in tech support for five years, first as a help desk technician and then as a second-tier desktop support employee. She lives in Portland, Oregon, where she spends her free time biking and reading. She also likes tinkering with computers, which mostly means pulling them apart to find out how they work, and then never remembering to put them back together.